THE
COMANCHE
INDIANS

THE JUNIOR LIBRARY OF
AMERICAN INDIANS

THE COMANCHE INDIANS

Martin J. Mooney

CHELSEA HOUSE PUBLISHERS
New York   Philadelphia

FRONTISPIECE: Comanche warriors on a horse-raiding expedition, painted by American artist Charles M. Russell in 1911

CHAPTER TITLE ORNAMENT: An image of a buffalo, adapted from a carving on a Comanche ceremonial rattle

Chelsea House Publishers

EDITOR-IN-CHIEF Richard S. Papale
MANAGING EDITOR Karyn Gullen Browne
COPY CHIEF Philip Koslow
PICTURE EDITOR Adrian G. Allen
ASSISTANT ART DIRECTOR Howard Brotman
MANUFACTURING MANAGER Gerald Levine
SYSTEMS MANAGER Lindsey Ottman
PRODUCTION COORDINATOR Marie Claire Cebrián-Ume

The Junior Library of American Indians

SENIOR EDITOR Liz Sonneborn

Staff for THE COMANCHE INDIANS

COPY EDITOR Margaret Dornfeld
EDITORIAL ASSISTANT Nicole Greenblatt
DESIGNER Debora Smith
PICTURE RESEARCHER Nisa Rauschenberg
COVER ILLUSTRATOR Vilma Ortiz

7 9 8 6

Library of Congress Cataloging-in-Publication Data

Mooney, Martin J.
   The Comanche Indians/by Martin J. Mooney.
      p.   cm.—(The Junior library of American Indians)
   Includes index.
   Summary: Examines the history, culture, and future of the Comanche Indians.
   ISBN 0-7910-1653-6
        0-7910-1957-8 (pbk.)
   1. Comanche Indians—Juvenile literature. [1. Comanche Indians.
2. Indians of North America.] I. Title. II. Series.
                                                          92-9932
E99.C85M66 1993   CIP
973'.04974—dc20   AC

CONTENTS

Skilled horsemen and warriors, the Comanches were masters of a vast region in the American Southwest known as the Comanchería.

CHAPTER 1

The Snake People

One day, long ago, two boys were playing a game. Both boys belonged to the same group of Indians, the Snake People. However, they were members of different bands within the group.

In the course of the game, one boy kicked the other in the stomach. The injured boy died. His band became furious. They wanted to attack the other band and take their revenge. Finally, an old man stepped forward. He reminded the angry crowd that the two bands were still one people. It would be wrong for them to fight among themselves.

7

Both sides knew the elder was right. But they also knew that they could no longer live together. One group agreed to move north. They became known as the Shoshones. The other group traveled south. They were later called the Comanches.

This is one story the Comanche Indians now tell to explain why they stopped living with their Shoshone relatives. Another such tale begins with the two bands hunting together. According to this tale, when a bear was killed, one hunter from each band claimed that he shot the fatal arrow. The bands split up when they could not agree which hunter was telling the truth.

Still another story holds that a terrible disease struck the Snake People. Many people fell ill and died. Those who did not decided that they could not survive if they stayed together.

No one knows which, if any, of these events actually happened. It is certain, however, that the Snake People became divided sometime around 1700. The Shoshones came to live in the mountains of present-day Wyoming and Montana. The Comanches eventually settled in what are now the states of Texas, New Mexico, Oklahoma, Colorado, and Kansas. This area became known as the *Comanchería*, or "the land of the Comanche."

The Comanchería stretched out over an area of more than 24,000 square miles. The Comanches' control over this vast territory was complete. They had many enemies, all of whom wanted to take over their land. But for many years the Comanches succeeded in fending off everyone who dared to challenge them.

The Comanchería was a land of many different features. Much of the area was flat and dry, but great rivers flowed through other parts. These included the Cimarron, the Pecos, the Brazos, and the Red.

The water of the rivers was often too dirty to drink, so the Comanches usually lived along the clear streams that fed into them. These streams also supported trees, which the Indians used to build shelter. However, the most important resource of the Comanchería was the thick, rich grass on which buffalo, elk, and deer grazed. These animals, especially the buffalo, were extremely important for the Comanches' survival.

Many years have passed since the Comanches followed the great herds of buffalo that used to wander the Great Plains of the

central United States. These buffalo herds are now gone. The Comanches, however, live on. Like the Snake People, they have faced many hardships throughout their history. But unlike their ancient ancestors, they were able to face these difficulties and survive as one people. ▲

Buffalo Drinking and Bathing at Night, *an 1837 painting by Alfred Jacob Miller. The Comanches obtained most of their food by hunting buffalo.*

A Comanche village
painted by George
Catlin, an artist who
visited the tribe in
the 1830s. The women
at the right are drying
buffalo hides, while
the men at the left are
playing a game.

CHAPTER **2**

The Comanchería

Whe the Indians first came to the Comanchería, their lives were very hard. Clear, drinkable water was scarce, and food could only be found with great effort. Often, especially in the winter or when hunting was bad, the old, the young, and the weak went hungry. Only the strong could survive.

The Comanches' harsh lives changed dramatically when they first acquired what would become their most treasured possession—horses. The horse is not native to North America. The animal was brought to the continent by Spanish soldiers, who first began to invade the Southwest in the 1540s. These soldiers were called *conquistadores*, the Spanish word for "conquerors." They had already conquered much of South America and Mexico. Now they were looking farther north for gold and other riches.

After failing in their search, some Spaniards settled among the Pueblo Indians living along a river known as the Rio Grande. For the most part, the Indians were treated cruelly by the Spanish. The Spanish enslaved the Pueblos, stole from them, and stole their land. They also forced the Indians to convert to Roman Catholicism, which was the Spaniards' religion.

This mistreatment continued for many years. Finally, after some 90 years of abuse, the Pueblos rose up in 1680. In what became known as the Pueblo Revolt, the Indians drove the Spanish from their lands. The Spanish were forced to flee so quickly that they left many of their possessions behind. The Indians had little use for most of these things. One great exception, however, was the Spanish soldiers' horses. The Pueblos and their Indian neighbors immediately saw the immense worth of these animals.

Soon the Comanches had horses of their own. Their harsh lives changed completely. On horseback, Comanche hunters could travel greater distances and find herds of wild animals more easily. They could now carry enough meat back to their camps to feed everyone. As a result, the Comanches became a healthier people. By the mid-1800s, their population swelled to more than 20,000.

The Comanches not only used horses, they used them well. They quickly became known throughout the Southwest as expert horsemen. Children learned to ride at an early age. As adults, both women and men spent much of their lives on horseback.

The Comanches were also skilled at obtaining the animals. Many of their horses were captured from the wild herds that roamed the plains. One of the ways they would catch wild horses was to lie in wait while a herd stopped at a watering hole for a drink. When the horses had finished drinking, the Indians would make their move. Sweeping down on the unsuspecting herd, they could easily capture the slow, waterlogged animals. The Comanches usually reserved this task for winter. At this time, the horses were likely to be underfed and too weak to resist capture.

The Comanches also stole horses from their enemies. In their view, this was not a crime. Just as they thought it was right to share with their friends, the Comanches considered it proper to take from their foes.

The buffalo meant even more than the horse to the Comanche way of life. The buffalo provided the Comanches with everything they needed. Its meat was the main component of the Indians' diet. Buffalo horns were made into bowls, cups, and spoons. The animal's bones were carved into tools, such as scrapers, needles, and awls. And its skin provided the material for the Comanches' clothing and dwellings.

Comanche buffalo hunters sometimes killed their prey by driving a great herd over the edge of a cliff.

The Comanches usually hunted with bows and arrows, although occasionally they used long spears called lances to kill their prey. Old men who could no longer hunt were responsible for making these weapons. Most were carved from wood, but some were made from the horns of buffalo and elk. The Comanches were very skilled at using these weapons. Even after they acquired guns from non-Indians, they preferred their lances and bows and arrows. Guns took too much time to reload and could not hit a target as accurately.

The Comanches tracked buffalo all year long, but the best time to hunt was in the late fall. At this time, the buffalo's coats were at their thickest, and the animals had fattened up in preparation for winter. A hunting party would set out in late November and not return until the cold and snow drove them back.

Unlike other Indians of the Great Plains, the Comanches did not have large organized hunts. They went out in small parties, and each man hunted for himself. On the Comanchería, there were many buffalo but fairly few people. To the north, where there were more people and fewer buffalo, hunts were more tightly controlled by hunt leaders.

When on the hunt, the Comanches lived in small groups called *bands*. Most people in a band were related, so bands were something like a very large family. But in one important way they were different. A person could choose to leave his or her band and join another at any time.

Comanche bands were scattered throughout the Comanchería. Bands on one terrain had one way of life, while bands in a different area developed another. Groups of bands that lived in a similar manner are now called *divisions*. Originally, there were six divisions among the Comanches.

The southernmost division was the Penatekas, or "Honey Eaters." The Penatekas were given this name because they lived in the only part of the Comanchería that had trees in which honeybees could build their hives.

In the middle of the Comanchería lived three divisions. These were the Nokonis (meaning Those Who Turn Back), the Tenawas (Those Who Stay Downstream), and the Tanimas (Liver Eaters). All three groups constantly traveled in the area between the Red and Colorado rivers in what is now north-central Texas.

North of these groups were the Yamparikas and the Kotsotekas. *Yamparika*

LOCATION OF COMANCHE DIVISIONS IN ABOUT 1750

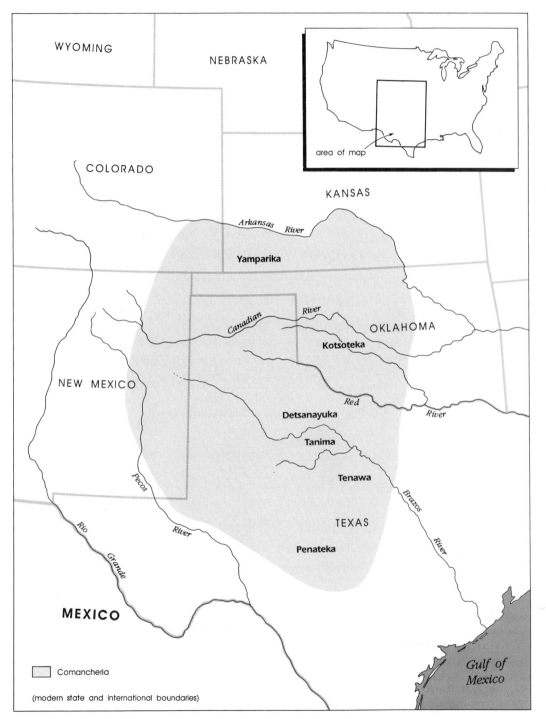

means "root eaters." The root of the yamp vine made up a large part of this group's diet. *Kotsoteka* means "buffalo eaters." All Comanches ate buffalo, but the Kotsotekas lived in the area where the largest buffalo herds were found. (In the 1800s, some Kotsotekas broke away and formed a seventh division—the Quahadis, or Antelopes.)

No one person made decisions for an entire division. Instead, each band followed its own leaders. These included the peace chief, the members of the band council, and the war chief. The peace chief was one of the oldest men of the band. His job was to give advice to anyone who came to him with a problem. The peace chief kept his post as long as people liked him, listened to his words, and followed his suggestions.

The band council was made up of all of the men in the band. Any member could speak at the council meetings, but the older men usually did most of the talking. The council made decisions about where the band should hunt, whether they should war against their enemies, and whether to ally themselves with other bands.

In times of war, the band council selected a war chief. To be chosen for this position, a man had to prove he was a brave fighter. He also had to have the respect of

A camp of the Quahadi band, photographed in the 1860s.

all of the other warriors in the band. While the band was at war, the war chief was in charge, and all warriors had to obey him. After the conflict was over, however, the war chief was not allowed to tell anyone what to do.

Dividing power among many people worked well for the Comanches. The system enabled them to occupy and control a huge territory. Their control over the Comanchería meant that they always had enough food for their ever-growing population. But it meant as well that they were always threatened by other peoples who wanted their land and its resources. The Comanches' survival, therefore, depended not just on the buffalo. It also depended on their ability to defend the plains where the great herds roamed. ▲

A Spanish painting of
a Comanche father,
mother, and child.

CHAPTER **3**

New Enemies

When the Comanches moved to the southern plains, they were not welcomed by the peoples of the region. They had to battle for the land that would become the Comanchería. Their conquests helped earn them their name. "Comanche" comes from a Ute Indian word *Kwuma-ci*, which can be translated as "one who fights all the time."

Among the tribes the Comanches battled were the Utes, the Pawnees, the Arapahos, the Kiowas, the Cheyennes, the Osages, and the Wichitas. But their greatest enemy was the mighty Apaches.

Like the Comanches, the Apaches were buffalo hunters. However, the Apaches were also farmers. They probably learned to grow crops such as corn and beans from the nearby Pueblo Indians. These foods supplemented whatever meat the Apaches brought in from the hunt.

In order to tend their farms, the Apaches were forced to stay in one place for long periods of time. This situation made them especially easy to attack. The Comanches, who traveled the plains freely, took advantage of this weakness.

Beginning in the early 1700s, the Comanches constantly raided Apache communities. (These communities were called *rancherías* by the Spanish.) Comanche raiding parties destroyed the Apaches' homes and stole their horses and livestock. They also took ranchería residents captive. By the end of the century, the Apaches had had enough of this warfare. Most fled westward into present-day New Mexico. The rest were driven south to the Rio Grande.

While the Comanches were fighting the Apaches, they were also meeting other peoples, who like themselves were foreigners to the area. To the north, the Comanches encountered Frenchmen. To the south, they found Spaniards.

Most of the Frenchmen who came to the southern plains were traders. Traveling down the Mississippi River from Canada, they brought all sorts of European goods the Indians had never seen—blankets, pots, metal tools, and, most important of all, guns. The Indians wanted these things very much. They were happy to trade their wares— mostly dried meat and buffalo skins—to obtain them.

The Spanish in the area had different aims. Most were searching for gold and other riches. But they also wanted the Indian peoples to give up their own religions and become Christians. Toward this end, many religious people known as *missionaries* arrived in the region. They set up communities known as missions, where they settled and tried to teach Indians about Christianity.

The Comanches traded with the Spanish as well as with the French. Given a choice, however, they preferred dealing with French traders. The French treated them as equals and were only interested in exchanging goods. The Indians found them easier to trust than the Spanish. The Spanish were not only trying to make the Indians give up their religion. They also had their eye on the Comanches' land.

After 1763, however, the Comanches no longer had a choice. In that year, the French

lost a war with British settlers. The war was fought on the East Coast of North America. After France's defeat, the British forced them to leave most of their settlements everywhere on the continent.

The Spanish quickly moved into the areas where the French had been. Suddenly, the Spanish controlled trade on both sides of the Comanchería. The Comanches were not happy with the new arrangement. They missed their French friends. They also missed the free trade they had had with the French. French traders had not hesitated to give the Comanches any goods they wanted. The Spanish, however, did not want to give the Comanches guns. They were afraid the Indians might use the weapons against them someday.

The Spaniards' fears were not foolish. Some Comanche bands made a habit of raiding their settlements. The Spanish government tried to end the fighting by making peace with individual bands. However, the Spanish did not understand that each band acted independently. When the settlers made a peace agreement with one band one week and were attacked by a different band the next, they felt as though they had been lied to. The Comanches saw no prob-

The Spanish built many missions on Comanche territory. The priests who came to live at these missions tried to convert the Indians to the Christian religion.

lem with the situation. As far as they were concerned, every band had the right to decide for itself who were its friends and who were its enemies.

One Spanish officer, Don Juan Bautista de Anza, tried to stop the attacks by following the Indian raiders and fighting them on their own territory. It was a daring decision. Spanish forces had tried battling the Comanches on the Comanchería before, but they had always failed miserably.

In the summer of 1779, Anza led his soldiers and some Ute and Apache warriors into the Comanchería. They came upon a group of Comanches and attacked. This time, the Spanish forces won. Their victory was a great blow to the Comanches. It told all their enemies that invading the Comanchería was possible.

The Comanches soon faced another disaster. Anza's soldiers had infected the Indians with smallpox, a deadly disease. Europeans had been falling ill with smallpox for centuries. Over that time, their bodies had developed ways of fighting off the smallpox germ. North American Indians, however, had never before been exposed to the disease. As a result, when Comanches caught smallpox, they were rarely able

A Spanish artist's depiction of a Comanche warrior from the Yamparika division.

to recover. In 1780 and 1781, the disease killed much of the Comanche population.

But even after the smallpox outbreak ended, the survivors feared for their lives. Their enemies knew that the Comanches were weakened by the many deaths. The

Comanches suspected that it was only a matter of time before another Indian tribe or Anza himself again tried to invade their lands.

Sensing they had no choice, a group of leaders from the Penateka and Kotsoteka divisions met with Anza in 1786. They asked for peace. Tired of the fighting and the raids, the Spanish officer was eager to hear them out. But Anza made it clear that he did not feel comfortable dealing with the large number of Comanche leaders at once. He wanted to talk one-on-one with a single leader. (This was the manner in which Europeans were accustomed to performing official business.) Even though the Comanches did not like the idea, they agreed to the officer's request. For the first time in their history, one man was chosen to speak for all of the Comanches. The Spanish called him Ecueracapa, which means Leather Jacket.

Ecueracapa and Anza agreed to end the fighting between their people. This peace lasted many years and benefited both sides. The Spanish helped the Comanches fight their enemies. They also traded with the Indians and even gave them food when hunting was bad. In return, the Comanches let

the Spanish travel safely through the Comanchería.

At peace with their greatest enemy, the
Comanches entered the 1800s still the masters of the Comanchería. But they hardly felt
secure. They knew from experience that no
matter how many allies they had, the future
would always bring new threats to them and
their lands. ▲

*George Catlin's sketch
of Comanche chiefs
smoking peace pipes.
The Comanches offered
pipes to visitors whom
they wanted as their
friends.*

CHAPTER **4**

Fighting Americans

By 1800, the Comanches were used to living near other peoples, both Indian and non-Indian. But their experience barely prepared them for their newest neighbors—Americans. The sheer number of Americans who would soon come to the Comanchería were to pose a threat unlike any the Comanches had ever known.

The United States was still a very young nation. It had gained its independence from England only in 1781. But it was growing fast, largely because of a land deal made by President Thomas Jefferson. In 1803, Jefferson bought a huge amount of land from

France. This tract, known as the Louisiana Purchase, included all of the land between the Mississippi River and the Rocky Mountains. The purchase doubled the size of the United States.

After Jefferson bought this land, Americans considered the Louisiana Purchase theirs. The Indians living there, however, did not see it that way. They had grown up on the land, just as their grandparents had, and their grandparents before them. It made no sense to them that France believed it could sell their land. Likewise, they thought the claim that the United States now owned it was absurd.

Some Americans started settling the Louisiana Purchase right away. But most of the first newcomers to the area were Indians from what is now the eastern United States. One of the reasons Jefferson bought the land was to provide a new home for these peoples.

The Eastern Indians did not want to move. They loved their territory just as the Comanches loved the Comanchería. They left only because they were forced to do so by the U.S. government. The government wanted to give the Eastern Indians' lands to white Americans. The plan was clearly unfair. But most people in the government had little respect for Indians and were untroubled about stealing their land.

During the 1830s, many Eastern Indians resettled in an area called Indian Territory. Originally, it included parts of present-day Oklahoma, Kansas, and Missouri. (As the years passed, Indian Territory became smaller and smaller. By the early 1900s, it comprised only part of what is now Oklahoma.)

The United States promised the Eastern Indians that Indian Territory would be theirs forever. But the Indian groups who already controlled the area did not think the United States had any right to make such an offer. Among these groups were the Comanches, who hunted on much of the land the Eastern Indians were settling. They considered the Eastern Indians intruders. And as they would have treated any intruders, the Comanches battled them fiercely.

Officials of the U.S. government stepped in to try and stop the fighting in Indian Territory. In 1834 and 1835, they helped make peace between the Comanches and several of their new Indian enemies. The Comanches were still not happy about these people living so close to the Comanchería. But, by and large, they respected the agreement.

At the same time, more Americans were making their way to the Comanchería. Most were traders or travelers on their way west to what is now California. Even though these people were not planning on settling on Comanche land, the Indians made it clear that they were not welcome.

The Comanches reserved most of their anger for their neighbors to the south—Texans. For many years, the Texan settlements close to the border of the Comanchería were a favorite target for Comanche raids.

In 1836, Texas won its independence from Mexico. The government of this new country—the Republic of Texas—decided that the Comanche attacks had to stop. The republic's first president, Sam Houston, wanted to make peace with the Indians. For a time, Houston had lived among the Cherokee tribe. There he developed a great respect for all Indian people. He felt that if the Texans treated the Comanches with honesty and fairness, the Indians would respond in kind.

Houston arranged a series of meetings with the Comanches that led to a peace agreement. According to the treaty, the Comanches would halt their raids on Texas. In return, the Texans promised they would stay off the Comanchería.

In the Council House Massacre of 1840, 12 Comanche leaders were brutally murdered by Texas soldiers.

Houston was pleased with the agreement. However, the Texas legislature—the part of the new government that made its laws—was not. When it did not pass the treaty into law, relations between the Comanches and the Texans grew even worse.

For the next few years, the southern plains of Texas were a violent and bloody place. Occasionally, the two sides would make peace, and the fighting would stop. But then some Texans or some Comanches would violate the peace agreement and attack their old enemies. The other side always retaliated, and the war would rage once again.

To protect itself against Comanche raids, the Republic of Texas formed the Texas Rangers. This special group of soldiers realized, like the Spanish before them, that the best way to fight the Comanches was to follow them into their own territory. Their assaults against the Indians on the Comanchería were very successful. In 1840, the Comanches were so worn down by the Rangers' attacks that 12 band leaders went to the council house at the Texas town of San Antonio to ask that the fighting stop.

In exchange for peace, the Texans demanded that the Comanches return all white captives they had taken in their raids. The most important band leader, Muguara, explained that this was impossible. The Comanches believed that captives belonged to the people who captured them. No one, not even the powerful Muguara, had the authority to order all the bands to turn over their prisoners.

This answer was unacceptable to the Texans. They did not know about Comanche customs and did not care to learn. They thought Muguara was merely being stubborn.

To scare the Comanches, the Texans brought a force of armed soldiers into the council house. They then told the leaders that they themselves would be held captive until all their white prisoners were released. The band leaders responded by jumping up and running for the door. Some were shot dead by the soldiers. The others pulled out knives and stabbed at the soldiers as they struggled to escape. But their weapons were no match for the Texans' firearms. When the shooting ended, all 12 leaders lay dead.

Soon all the Comanches learned of what had happened in the council house. The Council House Massacre, as the event became known, confirmed what the Indians had always suspected. The Texans were never to be trusted. The Comanches staged more raids than ever. And, as always, the Texas Rangers responded with attacks of their own.

In 1845, the Republic of Texas became the state of Texas. Suddenly, the Comanches' greatest enemies were no longer the citizens of a fledgling young nation. The Texans were now Americans with the backing of the U.S. government. The Comanches now faced their most powerful opponent ever. ▲

These Comanche, Cheyenne, and Kiowa men were confined in a prison in Florida when they refused to move to a reservation.

CHAPTER 5

Reservation Life

In the first three years after Texas became a state, more than 70,000 Americans flocked to the region. Many of them moved to the Comanchería. The number of whites traveling through Comanche territory grew even larger once gold was discovered in California in 1848. Thousands of miners ravaged the Comanchería as they rushed west in search of fortune.

The Comanches were outraged by the presence of these unwelcome newcomers. But even worse for the Indians was what the travelers left behind—more disease. The whites spread cholera and smallpox. Many

Comanches died after being infected with these deadly diseases.

By 1855, a large portion of the Comanchería had been taken over by Americans. In order to protect these settlers, the United States began to build forts there. The Comanches were now being treated as invaders on their own land.

Still, the U.S. government was not content. It wanted control of more Comanche land. Officials decided that the Indians should be confined to a small portion of the Comanchería. In return for agreeing to stay on this land, which the government called a *reservation*, the Comanches were promised that no whites would be allowed to settle on it.

The Comanches were not enthusiastic about the plan. However, in 1865 the borders of their reservation were set. It included most of what is now western Texas and western Oklahoma.

Even though the U.S. government considered this Comanche land, the citizens of Texas did not. Texan troops punished any Comanche who ventured into Texas to hunt. But, of course, they did nothing to white people who crossed into the Comanche reservation. Usually, these whites were attacked by the Indians.

Unhappy with their situation, Comanche leaders met with U.S. officials in 1867. A member of the Yamparika division named Ten Bears argued their case. He pleaded with the officials just to leave the Comanches alone. Well aware of the might of the U.S. Army, Ten Bears maintained that his people were not responsible for the vio-

In the mid-1800s, hundreds of wagon trains carrying white settlers rolled into the Comanchería.

lence on the plains. He said, "It was you (the government) who sent out the first soldier and we who sent out the second."

At the meeting, the officials offered the Comanches an even smaller reservation. No portion of it was in Texas, however. The U.S. government guaranteed that no Americans would be allowed to cross this reservation's borders.

The guarantee mattered little to the Comanches. The reservation was much too small—only 5,546 acres—and contained few buffalo to hunt. Most of the Comanche bands refused to settle there. Ten Bears again expressed the Comanches' discontent: "I was born where there were no enclosures and where everything drew a free breath. I want to die there and not remain within walls."

Those Comanches who chose to move found life on the reservation dismal. They could not feed themselves by hunting. Most Comanches did not want to farm, but even if they did, the soil was too infertile to grow many crops. They had no choice but to depend on the U.S. government to give them the basic necessities for life: food, clothing, and shelter. Only a few years before, the Comanches had been fully able to provide all of these things for themselves.

their fellow fighters fell dead, the Indians realized that Ishatai's power was not as great as he had claimed. The Comanche survivors retreated, disappointed that the Sun Dance could not save their people and their land after all.

The Comanches continued to raid white settlements occasionally. But the Adobe Walls battle was their last great effort to rid their world of Americans. The summer following the attack, the U.S. government announced that its troops would kill any Comanche who did not move to the reservation. Many Comanches then sadly admitted their defeat. They were weak, hungry, and ravaged by disease. Even the most spirited among them knew that reservation life would be better than another hard winter without food.

On the reservation, the Comanches learned that the U.S. government did not just want to take Indian land. It also wanted them to give up their way of life. Reservation officials called *agents* saw that Indians drew strength from their culture. The agents were afraid that the Indians might fight them again if they continued to feel powerful. To make the Indians less of a threat, agents said they could no longer live as their ancestors had.

Instead, the Indians had to live like their white neighbors. They were encouraged to become farmers, learn English, and convert to Christianity.

The Comanches did not want to act as white people did. They were proud of being Comanches. They wanted to continue being great hunters and to practice their own religion. The agents were insistent, however. Because the Indians relied on the food agents gave them, they often had to do whatever these officials said.

One of the many requests agents made of the Comanches was that they send their children to government-run schools. Comanche parents did not like these schools. But if they did not make their children attend them, the agents saw to it that their families had no food to eat.

Some Comanche children were sent to boarding schools. Many of these schools were far away from the reservation. Agents believed that if Indian children were away from the influence of their parents, they would eagerly take on white customs. But the agents were wrong. The Comanche students held on to their culture just as fiercely as their parents and grandparents had held on to their land.

continued on page 57